How to Influence Employees to Drive Safely & Save Money on Commercial Insurance

This guide was created with Vision Zero methodologies considered. This book is meant to not only equip management with the psychological know-how needed to sustainably influence behavioral change, but this book also serves as a comprehensive drivers policy guide.

Should your fleet have unique or unusual circumstances that are not considered in this guide, then please contact me. I fully anticipate this guide to evolve over time and as new concepts are produced and new studies are concluded.

This book is dedicated to all of those that are committed to saving lives through safer driving habits and community collaboration.

The Vision 8

Introduction 14

Organization Policy 15

Driver Responsibility 16

Risk Associated Behavior 18

Corrective Action 19

Captain of the Ship Philosophy 22

Safety Rules 23
   General 23
   Driving Policy 24
   Safe Driving Techniques 25
   Distracted Driving 28
   Transportation of Hazardous Materials 28
   Firearms/Weapons 29
   Fatigue Management 30
   Hours of Service (HOS) 30
   Driver Required Reporting 32
   Injuries and Illness 33
   Collisions 33
   Minor Collisions 35

Major Collisions   36

Driver Health Rules   37
Drug and Alcohol Policy   37
Definitions   39
DOT Requirements   42
DOT Regulated Workers Policy   43
  Prohibited Behaviors   43
  Use or Possession of Illegal Drugs
  43
  Use of Prescription Drugs   44
  Use of Non-Prescription Drugs   45
  Use or Possession of Alcohol   46
  Testing   46
  Testing Procedures   47
  Consent   48
  Collection and Chain of Custody
  48
  Testing Methods   49
  Other Alcohol-Related Conduct 50
  Notification   50
  Right to Re-Test   51
  Testing Categories   52
  Reasonable Suspicion   53
  Post-Incident   54
  Action on Positive Results   55
  Testing Guidelines   56
  Return-To-Work   57

Unannounced Follow-Up Testing
57

Positive Drug Test Results   57

Refusal to Submit to Testing   58

Confidentiality   58

Drug-Free Workplace Act
Compliance   59

Driver Violations Jeopardizing
Employment   60

Major Preventable Collisions   61

Suspension, Revocation, or
Cancellation of Driver's License   62

Drug and Alcohol Use, Abuse and
Testing   62

Driver Attire   63

Clothing   63

Safety Shoes   64

Personal Protection Equipment (PPE)
64

Safety Glasses   65

Hair Protection   65

Housekeeping Requirements   66

Electrical Equipment   66

HAZMAT – Hazardous Materials   67

Tire and Wheel Safety   67

Fire Safety   68

Spill Containment   69

Securing Cargo   71
Vehicle and Cargo Security / Key
Control   72
Side Guards & Truck Skirts   73

Pre-Trip and Post-Trip Responsibility 74
Pre-Trip CSA Inspection   74
Post-Trip Inspection   75
Pre-Documented Post-Trip
Inspection   77
Other Circumstances   78
Process For Vehicle Repairs   78
Post-Repair Certification   79
Retention   79
Roadside Inspections   80

Vehicle Safety Procedures   80
Entering or Exiting Vehicle Cabs And
Trailers   80
General Ladder Usage and Vehicular
Access   83
Lift Gate Safety   83
Starting or Parking the Vehicle   85
Cruise Control   85
Seat Belts   86
Unauthorized Passengers   87
Cell Phones and Texting   87
Radar Detectors   88

Headlights	88
Safe Backing	88
U-Turns	89
Security Rules	**90**
General	90
Security While Driving	90
Security During Energy Control Procedures	92
Security During Vehicle Maintenance	92
Fleet Management & Questions	**94**
Safety Gamification	**95**
Resources	**98**
Author – AJ T. Cole	**101**

The Vision

There are ample resources for organizations to utilize when it comes to preparing a driver policy and handbook, but something you won't likely find are instructions or outlines needed in order to comply with new and future Vision Zero regulations.

Vision Zero is a strategy to eliminate all traffic fatalities and severe injuries, while increasing safe, healthy, equitable mobility for all. Many cities and organizations across the world are adopting Vision Zero in an effort to not only save the lives of pedestrians and other drivers, but to also protect the lives of our world's commercial drivers.

Commercial drivers, tow-truck drivers, and other drivers on the road for business are at a significantly increased risk of being involved in a fatal crash. In fact, commercial motor vehicle drivers accounted for about 12% of all workplace fatalities and driving a truck is considered one of the most dangerous jobs in the United States.

The scariest part about this is that the death tolls are continuing to rise and how your drivers are navigating the roads is only one factor in the equation. When applying Vision Zero principles to driver policies there are a few things that change when we speak about traffic incidents. The most important change is when it comes to the way that we speak of these incidents. For example: We often say "accidents" – we have been colloquially conditioned to refer to all traffic-related incidents as accidents. However, not all incidents are in fact, accidents and by referring to an incident or crash as an accident it can do a disservice to the victim and how the incident is handled legally. By adjusting our language, we not only support victims, but we are supporting our trained drivers. In fact, 80% of commercial truck crashes were the fault of the other driver, not the trained driver.

For example, here is the difference between an incident and an accident, an **incident** would be if one driver were to rear end another vehicle while they were distracted by texting and driving. Whereas an **accident** would be if one driver were to rear end another vehicle because their brakes unexpectedly malfunctioned.

It is imperative that commercial drivers learn about and participate in Vision Zero efforts to set an example for the average driver. Big trucks and fleets can influence the rate of speed on highways. About 12% of all registered vehicles are commercial vehicles, which is great news for all of us because that number alone puts us above the tipping point of influence.

Psychologically – scientists at Rensselaer Polytechnic Institute found that when just 10% of the population holds an unshakable belief, their belief will always be adopted by the majority. Trained CDL drivers hold the power of influence and have seen it all during their time spent on the roads.

Commercial drivers are trusted by communities nationwide to protect themselves, other drivers, pedestrians, and bicyclists which makes commercial driving behavior the centerpoint of focus for the average population. This also means that commercial driver speeds hold a great deal of influence on other driver's behaviors.

As many of us have begun to witness or hear about in the news, traffic deaths have been on the rise in the U.S. for the last few years and experts have a few explanations as to what could be contributing to the rise. Some say it's due to an overall increase in driving, while others have tried to blame smartphone-holding pedestrians rather than the drivers themselves. However, a new study out from the National Transportation Safety Board declares there's a singular and unequivocal reason for the uptick in deaths: Speed is what's killing Americans.

Cities around the world are reducing speeds in an effort to protect pedestrians and bicyclists from the dangers of the roadways. Critics fear that lowering city speeds could increase the total trip time length, but that isn't the case. In fact, a lowered speed limit can achieve more uniform speeds and reduce dangerous midblock acceleration, while adding little to overall journey times. Research from Grenoble, France has shown that a speed limit of 18.64 mph rather than 31 mph only added 18 seconds of travel time between intersections .62 miles apart. In some cases, the reduction of speed actually reduced traffic congestion.

For example, in Sao Paulo, the speed limit on major arterials was lowered and it reduced congestion by 10% during the first month of implementation, while fatalities also dropped significantly.

Most importantly, slower speeds save lives. For every 1 mph reduction in vehicle speeds on urban streets results in a 6% decrease in traffic fatalities. There are scientific reasons why this is the case. One contributing factor is that driving at high speeds can result in tunnel vision and decreased depth perception for the driver whereas at lower speeds, drivers have a wider field of vision and are more likely to notice other road-users.

Even if a crash does occur that involves a pedestrian or cyclist, at lower speeds, the consequences will be less severe. A pedestrian has a 90% chance of survival if hit by a vehicle moving at 18.64 mph.

This decreases to 70% at 24.85 mph and less than 20% at 31 mph.

Driving at lower speeds also enables drivers to stop within a shorter distance, which can be critical for all drivers, but extremely crucial for drivers of larger vehicles. The stopping distance of a vehicle is a combination of the distance travelled during the driver's reaction time and the distance it takes for the car to stop after the brakes are applied. It is important to acknowledge that we are all human and with that means that we aren't perfect.

Therefore even in ideal situations, driver reaction times vary greatly with situation and from person to person between about 0.7 to 3 seconds or more. Some crash reconstruction specialists use 1.5 seconds. A controlled study in 2000 found average driver reaction brake time to be 2.3 seconds.

What is the reward for drivers that make these safer driving choices? A more robust local economy, more commercial driving opportunities as local economies grow and increase purchasing. Studies found that when streets are more inviting for walkers and cyclists, they are more economically successful than streets with high volumes of fast-moving traffic. Benefits include increased real estate value and higher spending on retail and services, boosting the local economy.

For example, in areas where streets were designed with narrower lanes that slowed traffic in the Mission District of San Francisco, nearly 60% of retailers reported increased spending by local people, and nearly 40% reported an overall increase in sales.

Lastly, with a speed-slowing infrastructure, cities may see positive trends in residents opting to walk or bike instead of driving. In fact, walking, biking, and getting fresh air leads to a healthier community. One study found that the United States could save $5.6

billion in health care costs if 1 in 10 adults started walking regularly.

This guide was developed for organizations to use as their own driver policy and it takes additional precautions to ensure safer driving that eliminates roadways fatalities and may reduce commercial insurance premiums.

Introduction

This guide is designed to equip drivers with the information needed to make safe decisions that protect them and reduce transport incidents. Chicken Communications is committed to helping drivers conduct all operations in a safe manner that protects and preserves both employees and the community. This means strict compliance with all applicable laws and recommended rules outlined in this guide will eliminate incidents, improve efficiencies, and ultimately reduce costs.

Please read this guide carefully and review this with your drivers. Together, we can eliminate transport incidents.

Organization Policy

Safety is a critical business objective and it is our belief that every collision, incident, and injury is preventable with the proper measures in place. Every employee and contractor representing the organization is required to work safely and responsibly as a condition of employment.

By building and maintaining a culture that is committed to safety will help us:
+ Prevent personal injury
+ Minimize property damage
+ Meet applicable regulations
+ Improve productivity
+ Protect organization assets
+ Reduce costs

Every commercial driver will receive a Federal Motor Carrier Safety Administration Handbook and will be required to return a signed acknowledgement to be filed in their driver qualification file.

Driver Responsibility

Your work practices lead the way toward creating a safer workplace and environment for yourself, your co-workers, and everyone you come in contact with while on the road. Your attitude towards safety is influential within the organization and community so it is important to demonstrate the highest level of maturity.

Conducting your work in a safe and responsible manner will help you:
+ Prevent personal injury
+ Prevent injury to co-workers and others on the road
+ Build a respected reputation
+ Gain organization-wide recognition

As a driver, you have a responsibility to:
+ Help fellow employees understand the importance of safe driving
+ Observe all safety rules, guidelines, and regulations
+ Correct any work-related hazards immediately and report such behavior
+ Report any unsafe conditions that may impact you and other drivers
+ Properly use the required personal protection equipment (PPE) and equipment
+ Report all incidents, collisions, injuries, or unusual events to your supervisor
+ Make safety and process improvement suggestions as you see fit
+ Participate in safety trainings and inspections
+ Keep a clean environment including within your vehicle

It is our view that employees conducting safe practices are more highly qualified and will be rewarded as such.

Risk Associated Behavior

When drivers fail to comply with safety guidelines and regulations it is considered risk-associated behavior and will not be tolerated. Safely conducting your job is a condition of employment.

An employee's behavior is considered risk-associated when the:
+   Employee has completed safety training, but violates these procedures in such a manner that it increases the risk of an incident
+   Employee has demonstrated a lack of maturity regarding safety instructions

Corrective Action

To ensure the safety of all employees and the public, when an employee has engaged in risk-associated behaviors it is the responsibility of management to take corrective action. The course of corrective action is dependent upon whether the employee has received any previous violations within a rolling three year timeframe.

The primary purpose of corrective action is to prevent future incidents and reduce risk-associated behaviors and is not intended to penalize employees for having a collision or injury.

The table below outlines the steps for corrective action for first, second, and third incidents involving risk-associated behaviors.

# of incidents in a	Corrective action

rolling 3yr period	
First	+ A manager will verbally review how the risk-associated behavior could have prevented + A document will be filed in the employee's personnel file outlining the counseling discussion + Provide remedial education and training to ensure the employee understands safety policies. Remedial training

	should take place immediately and any extensive training should be completed within 14 days of counseling
Second	+ A written warning will be sent to the employee to inform them that additional disciplinary action including termination may result from future risk-associa ted behavior + Additional remedial training to

	correct the risk-associated behavior and provide the manager with an action plan to eliminate risky behaviors + The employee will be suspended without pay for a period of three days
Third	+ Terminate the employee

Please note: Management may deviate from these steps if the risk-associated behavior is serious in nature and creates an imminent hazard to others. It is always advised to consult with Human

Resources prior to initiating any corrective actions outlined above.

Captain of the Ship Philosophy

While out on the road there may be unforeseen events that you may face where immediate action is necessary to correct potentially unsafe situations. This means that without fear of retribution, drivers have the right and responsibility to cease operations, including driving, when they feel they are unable to do so in a safe manner. It is the duty of management to be supportive and not pressure drivers to take unsafe risks.

When decisions are needed to be made quickly and time does not permit resolution through the ordinary process outlined in this guide, drivers are expected to take whatever actions are required to correct a potentially unsafe situation.

Only you the driver are capable of determining your ability to perform your duties safely and it is your responsibility to notify your supervisor immediately if there is a condition that prevents you from doing so. With the help of your supervisor, a safe solution will be determined. Unsafe conditions may include inclement weather conditions, illness, equipment failure, or driver fatigue.

If a driver proceeds under unsafe driving conditions, then they may be held personally accountable for risk-associated behavior. If a driver has any questions or needs guidance on these details, then please contact a supervisor.

Safety Rules

General

It is a condition of employment to work incident-free, which means that drivers should:

+ Get plenty of rest before coming to work to prevent driver fatigue – a common factor in many collisions
+ Abide by all local regulations and remain up to date on any regulatory changes
+ Familiarize your location's emergency action plans and review plans with their supervisor
+ Know all emergency contact information including your location's doctor, police, fire, and your supervisor – contact information is available by all organization telephones
+ Keep and maintain fire protection equipment in your vehicle at all times and know where fire extinguishers are at your facilities

+ Comply with all "No Smoking" policies and only smoke in the designated areas – this is a no smoking workplace
+ Inspect your vehicle prior to operation to ensure all signals and equipment are functioning properly
+ Attend all employee/driver safety meetings

Driving Policy

We are committed to the safety of our employees, customers, and community. Drivers are expected to operate organization-owned or leased vehicles. This organization requires all drivers to comply with the driving policy set forth below:

+ Drivers must respect the rights of other drivers, pedestrians, and bicyclists
+ Drivers must abide by all traffic laws and maintain a safe speed for the load that they are carrying and be capable of making

necessary adjustments when faced with adverse weather conditions

+ Organization vehicles are to be used solely for organization business
+ Vehicles and equipment are not to be operated in unsafe conditions
+ Drivers must be physically and metally fit to drive safely
+ Drivers may not use illicit drugs or alcohol prior to, or while operating a vehicle
+ Drivers must be licensed, qualified, and approved to operate any required equipment and/or vehicles

Safe Driving Techniques

Based on real data, here are techniques that are recommended to ensure safer transport:

+ Observe all traffic signs, and signals

+ Including, obeying all speed limits – deliberately driving in excess of the posted speed limit may result in corrective action up to termination
+ Do not tamper with your governor, any governor found to be tampered with will result in termination
+ Keep both hands on the wheel at all times to maintain control of the vehicle should you incur a front axel tire blowout
+ Remain on your designated route and do not venture – route deviations may result in unknown hazards and unforeseen consequences
+ Keep your eyes ahead and look ahead at about 12-15 seconds or about a quarter of a mile on the road – in densely populated areas, look at least two blocks ahead
+ Remain alert and react accordingly
+ Never stare at a single object for more than two seconds as your vehicle is traveling at great

distances while you are distracted – keep your eyes moving

+ When sunshine becomes distracting then clean your windshield, use sun visors, and consider wearing sunglasses to ease eye strain

+ Driving at the posted speed limit is permitted during optimum conditions, but slower speeds are expected in instances such as inclement weather, construction, and/or traffic – incrementally decrease speeds as conditions deteriorate

+ To ensure clear visibility and ample notice to other drivers on the road, engage turn signals for at a minimum of three flashes and re-scan your mirrors a final time to ensure clearance prior to changing lange, merging, or turning

+ Do not overdrive your headlights, meaning do not drive at speeds where you are unable to see hazards in enough time to come to a complete stop upon

illumination of the hazard by your
headlights
+ When faced with lane
encroachment where it is
necessary to avoid a potential
impact from opposing traffic,
always first look to go right in a
controlled and slow manner while
trying to remain on the roadway –
veering left may result in colliding
with oncoming traffic
+ When approaching an
intersection be prepared to stop
within your available site distance,
allowing cross traffic to
completely exit the intersection
before entering even when you
have the right of way, and never
change lanes while approaching
or driving within an intersection
+ Ensure your turn signals are
functioning properly and use
them at all times when planning to
make a turn and signal early
+ When making a right turn, control
traffic between you and the curb
+ When making a left turn, remain in
your lane until it is safe to make

the turn and clear along the left side of your vehicle – when making a wide turn, smaller vehicles unaware of your maneuver may slip alongside making them difficult to see

+ Be aware of any low clearances and know the height of your vehicle
+ Immediately notify your supervisor when any operating deficiencies are identified
+ Fully utilize all safety-related and collision prevention equipment provided to you
+ Always use three points of contact when exiting your vehicle and never walk or jump from the truck cab, the back of the vehicle, catwalk areas, or any other areas

Distracted Driving

Crash reports indicate that 80% of all collisions are caused by distracted driving and 25% of all fatal crashes are reported to be due to distracted driving.

Distracted driving crashes account for 41% of all fatal worker's compensation claims making it a highly dangerous activity.

Below is a list of the top driving distractions to avoid:
+ Operating your phone or handheld device
+ Programming your GPS
+ Eating
+ Adjusting the radio
+ Retrieving items from the floor or back seat
+ Smoking
+ Engaging in conversation with passengers
+ Reading billboards
+ Gawking at another crash scene
+ Communicating to other known pedestrians / drivers
+ Applying makeup
+ Reading notifications on your hands-free device

Transportation of Hazardous Materials

It is the responsibility of our drivers to understand and comply with the Department of Transportation (DOT) regulations governing the transport of hazardous materials. As required by the federal law, employees involved in transporting hazardous materials must receive the required training prior to initial assignment and every three years thereafter.

Regulations require that drivers have the ability to:
+ Recognize hazardous materials and their packaging along with the hazards of such
+ Check the accuracy of all labels and marking of hazardous materials including the bill of lading
+ Identify and utilize the correct placards required for the load
+ Understand and use all necessary emergency response information and instructions

- + Ensure that the load is properly secured and ready for transport prior to driving
- + Explain the methodology used to appropriately secure the particular load being transported
- + Protect yourself and others in the event of an emergency

Firearms/Weapons

The organization prohibits the possession or use of firearms on organization property or premises including within organization vehicles. Weapons include, but are not limited to firearms, knives, machetes, explosives, and other weapons that may cause harm to yourself or others. Any employee in violation of this policy will be subject to corrective action, up to and including termination.

Fatigue Management

Drivers shall not operate a vehicle nor shall management knowingly require or allow an employee to operate a vehicle or equipment while the driver is impaired by fatigue. Driver fatigue is included in the Captain of the Ship philosophy. Failure to comply with this policy will result in corrective action up to and including termination of employment.

Hours of Service (HOS)

As required by the Federal Motor Carrier Safety Regulations (FMCSR), drivers are required to document their hours of service (HOS) activities accurately. The organization will never instruct a driver to violate HOS regulations under any circumstances. Drivers are expected to:

+ Provide accurate HOS documentation – any intentionally fraudulent documentation will result in corrective action, up to termination
+ Comply with all HOS regulations, any violations will be considered a risk associated behavior and will

result in disciplinary actions as outlined previously

+ Abide by the strict 11-hour driving rule, 14-hour on-duty rule, and the 60/70-hour rules

+ Driving safely is the primary responsibility of the driver – if you are behind schedule, then remain behind schedule and do not attempt to make up for time by increasing speeds or taking other risk associated actions

+ Drivers are required to spend at least 15 minutes at minimum to inspect their vehicles and equipment prior to and at the conclusion of operation – specialized equipment may require ore inspection time

+ It is required that drivers submit manual duty logs and download on-board computer data on a daily basis or before their next departure

Driver Required Reporting

In addition to reporting collisions, work-related injuries, or unsafe working conditions, drivers are expected to report the following to their supervisor within 24 hours:

+ Any traffic citations both personal or on organization time
+ Convictions of any traffic violations
+ Receipt of any roadside inspections, regardless of the outcomes – in the event that a receipt is not provided, then request the inspector's business card and/or inspection case number
+ Loss of license or any other loss of the right to qualify as a commercial driver

Injuries and Illness

Should a work-related injury take place, then it is required that you immediately report the incident to your supervisor. Any failure to communicate so in a timely manner will result in corrective action up to termination.

In the instance that you are ill, contact your supervisor in advance of your shift or should you become ill while in the middle of a shift then alert your supervisor immediately. Working while ill is not safe for you or anyone around you, please be conscious your wellbeing and alert your supervisor at any early signs of illness.

Collisions

A collision is any occurence where a motor vehicle is involved in an incident which results in injury, death, or property damage unless the vehicle is properly parked.

In the event that a collision occurs:
+ If you are utilizing an onboard computer unit, then capture the "final minute data" prior to moving the vehicle
+ Move your vehicle safely off of the road and turn your ignition off
+ If qualified, give emergency medical care or receive any necessary medical care
+ Secure the scene and notify local authorities immediately
+ In accordance with FMCSR, display your reflective triangles
+ Complete the accident procedures
+ Report the collision to your supervisor immediately
+ Take photos of the scene of the collision as soon as possible and include all damage details and all four sides of vehicles involved – include license plate information and any property damage near the crash site along with photos

of the roadways and surrounding signage

+ Identify any possible witnesses and obtain their contact information
+ Make a note of any vehicle license plate numbers that were present at the time of the accident and may be a possible witness
+ Provide local authorities with the appropriate / valid license, registration, and insurance information
+ Never admit guilt, negligence, or speculate the causes of a collision and discuss the details only with the investigating authorities, managers, or those approved by the organization
+ Do not speak to any media and if you are approached by a media representative, then direct them to the organization's corporate communications department or your supervisor
+ Regulation requires alcohol and drug testing immediately following the collusion in the event that the

collision results in a fatality or if our driver received a citation coupled with either emergency medical treatment away from the scene or a vehicle being towed
+ A collision will be considered preventable when the results show that the driver engaged in any risk-associated behaviors or by not driving defensively

Minor Collisions

Any preventable minor collisions that occur within a rolling 36-month timeframe will result in the following corrective actions:
+ 1st Offense – driver will receive counseling from their supervisor, written reprimand, complete remedial driving training, and satisfactory check ride required
+ 2nd Offense – driver will receive a 3-day suspension without pay, written reprimand, complete remedial driving training, satisfactory check ride, and an

employee action plan will be created to remedy risk associated behaviors
+ 3rd Offense – termination

Major Collisions

Should a major collision be deemed preventable, then the employee responsible for the collision will be terminated. A collision is considered major in the event that any of the following occurrences take place:
+ Collision resulting in a fatality
+ Emergency medical treatment away from the scene is required
+ Damage exceeds $30,000

Collisions will be deemed "non-preventable" if the driver was not engaging in any risk-associated behaviors and was properly applying defensive driving techniques ensuring they took all necessary precautions to avoid the collision. The involved driver has the right to request a formal collision review board within three days of receiving the preventability decision. If drivers have any questions, then they should review these with their supervisor.

Driver Health Rules

Drug and Alcohol Policy

We are committed to maintaining a drug-free workplace. Drug and alcohol abuse impairs judgement and pose a direct risk and significant threat to the safety of both employees and the community. This drug and alcohol policy applies to all employees and organization representatives and is vital in ensuring the organization is safely operating. All employees are expected to adhere to these guidelines.

The term "employee" includes all regular full-time, part-time, temporary, casual, leased, or contracted doing business on behalf of the organization. All contract and supplier personnel are required to adhere to the policy and expected to abide by our organization's rules, but will be referred to their own employers whenever testing is indicated.

Employees are subject to the Department of Transportation rules on drug and alcohol abuse and enforced by the Federal Motor Carrier Safety Administration and/or the Federal Transit Administration. Additionally, employees must also comply with our organization Drug and Alcohol Policy. We reserve the right to revise this policy at any time. Our organization complies with and may exceed regulations placed by local, state, and federal authorities.

All candidates for employment must successfully pass a post-offer drug screening prior to their start date and they do not, then their offer of employment will be withdrawn.

The illegal manufacture, dispensing, distribution, possession, sale, or purchase of any controlled substance is prohibited at all times. Employees may not be under the influence of alcohol or have any illicit drugs in their system while on organization property or while performing any work for the organization.

Should an employee test positive on a drug or alcohol test, it will be considered proof of policy violation. An alcohol test will be deemed positive if it indicates a blood-alcohol level of .02% or greater. Employees who violate this policy are subject to corrective action, up to termination. Contact your supervisor for guidance and questions related to this policy.

Definitions

Alcohol – Any substance capable of being consumed containing ethanol or ethyl alcohol is an alcoholic beverage. Under the Tex. Alco. Bev. Code § 1.04 alcohol beverage means "alcohol, or any beverage containing more than one-half of one percent of alcohol by volume, which is capable of use for beverage purposes, either alone or when diluted."

Organization Property – Means any and all property, real, personal or otherwise, tangible or intangible, which is transferred or conveyed to the Organization (including all rents, income, profits and gains therefrom), which is owned or held by, or for the account of, the Organization.

Risk-Associated Behaviors – Any behavior that potentially exposes people to harm, or significant risk of harm.

Designated Employee Representative (DER) – The employee in a workplace who is authorized to determine when a safety-sensitive employee, as defined by federal transportation safety laws, may be removed from duty.

Drugs/Controlled Substances – In this policy, it refers to the use of any drug regulated under the Federal Controlled

Substances Act, and includes all drugs available by prescription.

Medical Review Officer (MRO) – A person who is a licensed physician and who is responsible for receiving and reviewing laboratory results generated by an employer's drug testing program and evaluating medical explanations for certain drug test results.

On-Duty / Duty – Includes all time performing or in readiness to perform any work for the organization.

Regulated Employee – A covered employee or maintenance-of-way employee who performs regulated service for a railroad subject to the requirements of this part.

Safety-Sensitive Functions – The requirements of this policy are often dependent upon an individual's performance of a "safety-sensitive" function. A driver is considered to be performing a safety-sensitive function during any period in which he or she is actually performing, ready to perform, or immediately available to perform any safety-sensitive functions.

Safety-sensitive functions may include:

+ Time spent at a carrier or shipper plant, terminal, facility, or other property, or any public property, waiting to be dispatched, unless the driver has been successfully relieved of duty by the organization

+ All time inspecting equipment as required by regulation 49 CFR 392.7 and 49 CFR 392.8 or otherwise inspecting, servicing, or conditioning any commercial motor vehicle at any time

+ All time spent operating or at the driver controls of a commercial motor vehicle

+ All time in or upon any commercial motor vehicle except, time spent resting in a sleeper berth conforming to the requirements of regulation 49 CFR 393.76

+ All time spent loading or unloading a vehicle, supervising, or assisting in the loading or unloading, attending a vehicle being loaded or unloaded, remaining in readiness to operate a vehicle, or in giving or receiving receipts for shipments loaded or unloaded

+ All time repairing, obtaining assistance, or remaining in attendance upon a disabled vehicle

Substance Abuse Professional (SAP) – A person who evaluates employees who have violated a DOT drug and alcohol program regulation and makes recommendations concerning education, treatment, follow-up testing, and aftercare.

Serious Incident – Any work related incident or accident that requires any person to receive professional medical care or treatment.

Accident – An unavoidable incident that occurs when an employee has not engaged in any risk-associated behavior and therefore could not avoid the incident in any way.

DOT Requirements

The US Department of Transportation (DOT), Federal Motor Carrier Safety Administration (FMCSA), and the Federal Transit Administration (FTA), acting to implement a federal law called the Omnibus Transportation Employee Testing Act have adopted regulations requiring our organization to implement and abide by an employee drug and alcohol policy for commercial motor vehicle operators and transit workers. Please refer to the DOT Regulated Workers' Drug and Alcohol Policy for guidance.

DOT Regulated Workers Policy

Prohibited Behaviors

All employees are prohibited from using illegal drugs whether on or off duty and may be subject to restrictions regarding their use of prescription drugs and over-the-counter drugs. Employees may not use alcohol while working or while on organization premises except as described below.

Use or Possession of Illegal Drugs

The use, possession, manufacture, distribution, sale, attempted sale, or other involvement with illegal drugs by any employee is prohibited and will result in corrective action, up to termination of employment.

The use of any prescription medication that is illegal to use or possess in the United States or that is prescribed for another person is prohibited by our organization policy.

The use of "medical marijuana" and synthetic marijuana is prohibited by federal law and by this policy. Our organization will not accommodate medical marijuana unless affirmatively obligated to do so by law.

Use of Prescription Drugs

A driver cannot take a controlled substance or prescription medication without a prescription from a licensed practitioner. Prohibited drugs may also include prescription medications, under some circumstances.

If a driver uses a drug identified in 21 CFR 1308.11 (391.42(b)(12)) or any other substance such as amphetamine, a narcotic, or any other habit forming drug, The driver is medically unqualified.

However, according to the FMCSA, there is an exception: The prescribing doctor can write that the driver is safe to be a commercial driver while taking the medication. In this case, the Medical Examiner may, but does not have to certify the driver.

Any anti-seizure medication used for the prevention of seizures is disqualifying.

The Medical Examiner has 2 ways to determine if any medication a driver uses will adversely affect the safe operation of a CMV:

1. Review each medication - prescription, non-prescription and supplement
2. Request a letter from the prescribing doctor

Per this policy, the use of prescription medication is prohibited when:

+ Medication is not prescribed for the employee
+ Employee takes more than the prescribed dosage
+ Medication adversely causes the employee to become impaired or unfit while on duty
+ Employee is a driver or machine operator and the medication warns user to avoid driving or operating machinery
+ Medication is not approved in accordance with DOT regulations for use while on duty
+ The use of methadone or marijuana always disqualifies a

driver from performing DOT
regulated safety-sensitive work

Use of Non-Prescription Drugs

The use of non-prescription /
over-the-counter drugs is prohibited
when:

+   Medication causes the employee
    to be impaired or unfit for duty
+   Employee is a driver or operates
    machinery and the drug warns
    the user to avoid driving or
    operating machinery

The use of non-prescription /
over-the-counter drugs that contain
alcohol are subject to the same
restrictions our organization places on
the use of alcoholic beverages while
working. Safety-sensitive and regulated
employees must not take any drug that
contains alcohol within four hours
before duty.

Prohibited use of non-prescription
drugs will result in corrective action, up
to termination of employment.

Use or Possession of Alcohol

The use or possession of alcohol by any employee is prohibited while on organization property and may be grounds for corrective action, up to termination.

Exceptions to this rule may be made by management for the use of organization-sponsored events. Employees who choose to consume alcohol at such events are expected to exercise good judgement and refrain from becoming intoxicated or impaired.

Testing

Employees are subject to certain categories of drug and/or alcohol testing as described below:

Our organization may test for some or all of the following substances:

+ Amphetamines, including methamphetamine, MDMA (ecstacy) MDA, MDEA)
+ Barbiturates (sleep aids, Nembutal)
+ Benzodiazepines (Xanax, Zoloft)
+ Cocaine (crack, blow)
+ Marijuana (hash, weed, cannabis, CBD, including synthetic marijuana, K2, spice)
+ Opiates and synthetic opiates (heroin, morphine, oxycodone, methadone)
+ Phencyclidine (PCP, angel dust)
+ Propoxyphene (Darvon)
+ Alcohol

Note: Other substances may be added to this list. These policies shall be applied in a manner that complies with federal, state, and local laws. If this policy is inconsistent with the applicable laws of a particular location, then local managers and human resources personnel will be trained to ensure the policy is administered in a manner that is in compliance with the law.

Testing Procedures

All organization-utilized testing facilities, collection sites, and drug testing laboratories are expected to comply with state law and abiding by the regulatory guidelines published by the US Department of Health and Human Services (DHHS) for federal workers. Our organization's testing practices ensure:

+ Privacy of all individuals being tested
+ Non-discriminatory testing methods
+ Integrity of specimens

Consent

All employees are required to provide written consent agreeing to the organization drug testing policy. Drug testing will not be administered on a sample without written consent. A person's refusal to submit to a proper test will be viewed as insubordination and will lead to corrective action, up to termination. Any attempts to tamper with, substitute, adulterate, dilute, evade, or otherwise falsify a test, or failing to appear at the testing location promptly is considered a refusal to submit to a test. Our organization will pay the costs of all drug and/or alcohol testing that is required of employees.

Collection and Chain of Custody

Employees being tested will be asked to provide a test sample by the site collection person. Procedures for the collection of specimens will allow for reasonable privacy. Urine specimens will be tested for temperature and may be subject to other verification tests to detect tampering. The site collection person and person being tested must maintain chain-of-custody procedures for specimen collection, shipment, and storage.

Chain-of-custody (CoC), as it pertains to this policy is the chronological documentation that records the sequence of custody, control, transfer, analysis, and disposition of specimens.

Testing Methods

All drug test samples will be screened using an immunoassay and all presumptive positive drug tests will be confirmed using gas chromatography/mass spectrometry (GC/MS). All tests will be conducted by a laboratory certified by the Federal Substance Abuse and Mental Health Services Administration (SAMHSA).

Typically, alcohol tests will be conducted using breath or saliva and will be confirmed immediately at the collection site. Tests will only seek information regarding the presence of drugs and alcohol and will not test for any medical conditions.

Other Alcohol-Related Conduct

No driver tested under the provisions of this policy who is found to have an alcohol concentration of 0.02 or greater, but less than .04 shall perform or continue to perform safety-sensitive functions for an employer, including driving a commercial motor vehicle. Nor shall the organization employer permit the driver to perform or continue to perform safety-sensitive functions until the start of the driver's next regularly scheduled duty period, but not less than 24 hours following administration of the test. The successful passing of another test is required prior to the employee returning to duty.

The organization shall not take any action under this part against a driver based solely on test results showing an alcohol concentration of less than 0.04. This does not prohibit an employer with authority independent of this part from taking any action otherwise consistent with the law.

Notification

Any employee who tests positive for drugs will be notified by a Medical

Review Officer (MRO) and given the opportunity to provide any legitimate reasons they may have to explain the positive drug test. If the individual provides the MRO with an explanation that the positive drug test result is caused by factors other than the use of illegal drugs, the MRO will report the test as negative to the organization. Otherwise, the MRO will verify the test as positive.

The MRO may also review test results that are suspected to be diluted, substituted, or adulterated, and verify those tests. A negative dilute result will cause the organization to ask the employee to submit to a second test collection immediately and without prior notice. The organization may decline to hire any individual who submits a second dilute test result in a single testing incident. Employees who submit negative dilute results will be required to submit a second specimen for testing without prior notice and may be asked to submit to hair and/or oral fluids test in addition to, or instead of, a second urine sample. Individuals will be provided a copy of the notice of their own positive test results upon written request to the Substance Abuse Prevention & Control Department, or as required by law.

Right to Re-Test

An employee whose test is verified positive for the presence of drugs or alcohol may request that his/her original test sample be sent to an independent certified laboratory for a second confirmatory test, at the individual's expense.

Requests for re-tests must be made promptly, generally within seven days of being notified of the positive test result, unless the positive results indicate a fast-metabolized drug. In the instance that an employee tests positive for a drug known to metabolize within 48 hours, the re-tested employee will be subject to a hair follicle test. Tests that fail to reconfirm will be disregarded and the individual will be reimbursed for the cost of the test.

A request for re-test will not prevent the organization from suspending, transferring, or taking other action with respect to the employee's work assignment, pending the results of the re-test.

<u>Testing Categories</u>

The following testing categories constitute the organization's drug and alcohol testing program:

Pre-employment – All candidates for employment must successfully complete a post-offer pre-employment drug screening with a verified negative (non-dilute) test result.

Universal Testing – Except where such testing is prohibited by state or local laws, all employees not subject to random testing under DOT regulations will be subject to drug testing under the organization's Universal Testing category.

Employees will be selected at random by a computer program and/or a third-party service. All employees in the random testing pool have an equal chance of being selected for testing each time a selection is made. Tests will be conducted throughout the year and spread in such a manner as to make test dates unpredictable.

The designated location contact will receive a confidential list of employees selected for testing. Selected employees must report to the collection site for testing immediately upon notification.

Employees who refuse to submit to testing will be immediately terminated. Similarly, employees who fail to report to the collection site within an appropriate amount of time will be immediately terminated, unless it is concluded that the delay was caused by circumstances beyond the employee's control, which will be determined by location management and human resources.

Reasonable Suspicion

All employees at all locations are subject to Reasonable Suspicion testing for drugs and/or alcohol when it appears that the employee may be under the influence and/or is otherwise in violation of this policy. Only specifically trained supervisors may determine when Reasonable Suspicion testing is warranted.

Supervisors that have been specifically trained are able to recognize the signs of the misuse of drugs and/or alcohol. They are trained to make judgements based on physical appearance, body odors, performance, behavior, and/or other indicators.

Approval from a human resources representative is required prior to conducting any drug test under the Reasonable Suspicion policy.

Post-Incident

Employees whose acts, or failure to act, appear to have caused or contributed to an incident (or accident) may be asked to submit to post-incident testing.

When is testing required?
+ A crash involving a fatality
+ A crash resulting in an injury that required someone to be treated away from the scene
+ One or more vehicles needed to be towed
+ Driver was cited for traffic violations

No driver required to take a post-crash alcohol test under this policy may use alcohol for eight hours following the incident, or until they undergoes a post-crash alcohol test, whichever occurs first. (Violation 382.209.)

Action on Positive Results

In the event that a driver test indicates an alcohol concentration level of .02 or greater, the individual tested will be immediately removed from any safety-sensitive functions and will be prohibited from operating equipment or a motor vehicle, including personal vehicles. That individual will also be responsible for arranging transportation home or back to their workplace for further testing. If the individual refuses to comply and continues to attempt to operate a motor vehicle, then the organization will take appropriate measures to discourage the individual from doing so, including contacting local law enforcement officials. Any individual who fails to cooperate with any of the procedures outlined in this policy will also be subject to correction actions including up to termination.

Employees must:

+ Remain available for additional testing until they have been tested or until 32 hours has passed since the incident
+ Alert management on where they may be contacted
+ Not use any drugs or alcohol until they have been tested
+ Make themselves available for testing when they leave the scene of an incident

Employees who do not remain readily available for additional testing will be considered as refusals and will be terminated from employment with the organization.

Testing Guidelines
+ Alcohol testing should be conducted within two hours of the incident
+ Alcohol testing cannot be conducted if more than eight hours have elapsed since the incident
+ Drug testing must be conducted immediately following the

incident, but no later than 32 hours after the incident
+ If testing cannot be conducted within the required time limits, a Post Accident Documentation Form must be completed
+ A moving violation must have been given (fatality excluded) to the driver in regards to the crash

Return-To-Work

Drug testing is required for all non-DOT regulated employees who are returning from a leave of absence of 90 days or longer. Return-to-work testing applies, regardless of type of leave taken. Common extended leaves that this applies to may include military, maternity, medical, and personal.

Unannounced Follow-Up Testing

Our organization's Drug and Alcohol Policy requires employees who have successfully completed a drug and/or alcohol rehabilitation program to be subject to unannounced testing for two years following the completion of the program (up to five years for DOT-regulated employees).

Positive Drug Test Results

If an individual's drug test result is positive, then they will be contacted by a Medical Review Officer. The MRO will review the test results with the individual to determine alternative explanations for the positive results (certain over-the-counter and prescription drugs taken during that time may result in a positive result medically explainable).

The organization will not be informed about a positive test result until the MRO has confirmed the positive result and conducted all MRO procedures on the test. However, if the individual does not return the MRO's calls, the MRO will verify the test as positive and report the result to the organization. The MRO may also ask our organization for assistance in contacting a current employee. Employees who test positive for drugs or alcohol will be subject to corrective action, up to termination.

Refusal to Submit to Testing

An employee who refuses to submit to required drug or alcohol testing will be considered to have failed the required test. Attempts to substitute, dilute, adulterate, and/or tamper with any test sample are treated as a refusal, as is submission of more than one dilute specimen on a particular testing occasion. Refusals will result in immediate termination or the withdraw of an employment offer.

Confidentiality

Management is expected to maintain confidentiality and respect employee privacy at each phase in the testing process. Test results will be shared within the organization and its agents only on a need to know basis and test results will not be released outside the organization except with the written consent of the individual or as required by law or legal process.

Drug-Free Workplace Act Compliance

Our organization is subject to the requirements of the federal Drug-Free Workplace Act of 1988 by virtue of its contracts to provide goods to the United States government. As part of the organization's commitment to comply with that law, our organization will provide education and training to employees and supervisors as described below. In addition, our organization requires employees who are convicted of a crime involving drug-related activity occurring in the workplace to notify his or her manager within five days. A conviction means there has been a finding of guilt, including a guilty plea or no contest, or imposition of sentence by any judicial body. The organization must then report the conviction to the contracting agency or government entity, in accordance with federal law. Within 30 days of the date it learns of the conviction, our organization will discipline the employee.

Driver Violations Jeopardizing Employment

Drivers all begin their employment based on their prior three-year driving record. Maintaining a safe record is the basis for continued employment.

If any of the following violations occur, then drivers may be terminated:
+ Speeding, a driver found to be driving 15 miles per hour or more

over the posted speed limit will be terminated
+ Possession of alcohol in a vehicle violates local, state, and/or Federal Motor Carrier Safety Regulations (FMCSR)
+ Driving while under the influence of drugs or alcohol
+ Violating traffic law or driver safety guidelines in connection with a fatal crash
+ Driving while physically impaired
+ Violating out-of-service orders
+ Driving with an expired license
+ Improper and/or erratic traffic lane changes
+ Tailgating or following a vehicle too closely
+ Reckless or careless driving as defined by the applicable laws including any offensive driving or willful and/or lackadaisical disregard for safety of people or property

Additional violations are also included regarding incidents in connection with a collision:

+ Leaving the scene of a crash
+ Acts directly contributing to the cause of a collision
+ Violation of applicable laws relating to motor vehicle traffic control (other than vehicle weight, vehicle defect violations, and parking)

Major Preventable Collisions

Drivers found responsible for or contributing to a major preventable collision will be considered for termination. A preventable collision is a traffic incident where the driver did not practice safe driving techniques and do everything possible to avoid the incident, which resulted in:

+ Fatality
+ Medical treatment for anyone involved in the incident requiring someone to be taken away from the scene
+ More than $20,000 in total property damage

+ One or more vehicles being towed from the scene or damage preventing any involved vehicle from leaving the scene of the crash under its own control

Suspension, Revocation, or Cancellation of Driver's License

Drivers may be terminated immediately if the annual review of their Motor Vehicle Registration (MVR) indicates that the driver's license is currently suspended, revoked, or cancelled, including for administrative reasons (non-safety related) or if their MVR lists drug charges or a felony while driving a personal or commercial vehicle.

Drug and Alcohol Use, Abuse and Testing

Any driver who receives any motor vehicle action for driving under the influence, or driving while intoxicated while on organization business, must report the motor vehicle action or citation to their supervisor within 24 hours.

DOT regulated employees who receive a DUI/DWI citation or other motor vehicle action outside of working hours on personal time are required to report this to their supervisor within 24 hours of the action or citation.

Our organization has the right to suspend driving privileges or terminate any employee whose position requires driving a motor vehicle, if that employee received a DUI or DWI motor vehicle action.

Driver Attire

Clothing
+ Proper dress is required while on duty
+ Wear uniforms as directed by your location supervisor

- + The shirttail must be tucked inside trousers
- + Appropriate PPE (gloves, eye protection, reflective vests, etc.) is required when performing hazardous tasks and/or as directed by your supervisor
- + Avoid wearing jewelry including rings, watches, bracelets, and chains – jewelry can get caught in machinery and vehicle components
- + If chemicals or fuel are spilled on your clothing, wipe it off as soon as possible or if excessive, change your clothing
- + Wear high-visibility, reflective vests when working in high traffic areas including by the roadside at collision or breakdown sites

Safety Shoes

Employees are required to wear appropriate safety shoes whenever on duty driving, in the vehicle, or while operating in a hazardous work area. Safety shoes must be:

+ Organization-approved, consult your supervisor for a list of approved vendors
+ Lace-up style with ankle protection and a minimum of 6" in high boot
+ Enhanced slip, resistant with toe protection and in good condition
+ Approved overshoes may be used during extreme weather conditions
+ Western or slip-on styles are prohibited

Personal Protection Equipment (PPE)

+ PPE must be worn when working with various hazards – review your location's specific requirements with your supervisor
+ To guard against frostbite and wetness, additional footwear must be worn
+ During cold weather while working outside gloves, jackets, and additional footwear are required

Safety Glasses

Safety glasses are mandatory for anyone visiting or working within the work areas of maintenance facility/shop. Glasses are also required wherever maintenance work is being performed or wherever there is a reasonable risk of an eye injury.

Any employees who may be exposed to hazards in their daily work routine such as securing tarps to flatbeds are required to wear eye protection.
+ All safety glass frames and lenses must meet the requirements established by the American National Standards Institute and be marked Z-87 approved
+ All safety glasses must have side-shields attached for wrap around side coverage

Hair Protection

Hair that touches the shoulders must be secured completely above the shoulders to prevent it from being caught in moving machinery, vehicles, or components.

Housekeeping Requirements

Electrical Equipment

All electrical equipment including extension cords and tools must be maintained in excellent condition (no cuts or abrasions) and should be equipped with a three-prong grounding plug or be internally grounded.

Drivers should:
+ Report any defective equipment immediately to your supervisor
+ Not try to repair any damaged electrical equipment
+ Take the equipment out-of-service immediately until it can be

replaced or repaired professionally
+ Immediately report any electrical system problems including missing junction box plates and switch or outlet covers
+ Tag defective electrical equipment as out-of-service and do not use until properly repaired

HAZMAT – Hazardous Materials

Unless otherwise approved, no placarded HAZMAT vehicles are allowed inside the maintenance shop unless they have been properly cleaned, prepped, and are free of residual hazardous materials and/or vapors.

Tire and Wheel Safety

Drivers should:
+ Check tire pressure daily – failure to do so can result in extreme vehicular fires and may contribute to a collision

- Tires should be maintained at the recommended pressure that is posted on the exterior of the vehicle
- Only operate vehicles with properly inflated tires
- Tires should be checked daily for proper tread depth and to ensure that no tire sidewall damage exists (gouges, bulges, tread separation, cuts, nails)
- Check wheel lugs for tightness, daily
- Never climb on tires or wheels – greasy surfaces contribute to slips, trips, and falls
- Evaluate and ensure there are no signs of oil/wheel seal problems
- Only inflate tires while in a tire cage – if any tire is identified on the service island as 10+ PSI lower than specified, it must be removed, repaired, and inflated in the tire cage

Fire Safety

Drivers are required to know the location of all fire protection equipment and fire extinguishers in both their facility and vehicle.

+ Fire extinguishers within vehicles must be securely mounted and labeled – they may not store or sit loosely
+ A minimum of 5 B L is rated for non-hazmat cargo
+ For equipment demonstrations, consult your supervisor
+ Never stack, store, or block any extinguisher – this blocks user access and is illegal
+ Never attempt to connect portable accessories into the vehicle's electrical system unless it is equipped with a standard 12V plug – improper connections can lead to electrical fires
+ Most vehicle fires are the result of problems with electrical equipment, wheel or brake

problems, or running on flat or improperly inflated tires

+ Heating devices such as hot plates are prohibited for use in motor vehicles
+ Use caution with engine compartment fires – raising the hood may feed oxygen to the fire
+ Tire and wheel fires generate high heat – if safely possible, get the vehicle off of the road, disconnect your trainer, and try to cool the fire with a nearby water supply – a fire extinguisher will quickly exhaust and will cause the fire to flame up again
+ In the event of a vehicle fire, contact local authorities immediately for assistance

When handling a fire extinguisher, OSHA recommends the PASS method.
P – Pull the pin
A – Aim low at the base of the fire
S – Squeeze the handle
S – Sweep side to side

Spill Containment

A spill is defined as any accidental discharge of petroleum products, hazardous materials, or hazardous waste.

The first person(s) to identify a spill must take immediate action to control the leakage by stopping it at the source. Do not move attempt to move the vehicle. While working to correct the spill, be sure to wear the appropriate PPE.

Examples of how to control a spill include:
+ Immediately shutting off the vehicle ignition
+ Shutting off the crossover line valve
+ Plugging any holes in the tank and/or place a container to catch the spill

Take immediate action to prevent the spill from reaching any waterways, groundwater, storm sewers, or soil. Different types of spills and the location of the spill may be require different containment procedures.

If a spill is **able to be contained** by the driver, then the following actions must be taken:
+ Use vehicle spill kit supplies to contain spill
+ Notify facility emergency coordinator

If a spill is not able to be contained by the driver, then the following actions must be taken:
+ Immediately notify facility emergency coordinator
+ Contact the organization's environmental services team
+ Call the fire department and/or an approved emergency response contractor or insurance carrier

Any supplies that are removed from the Vehicle Spill Kits must be immediately replaced after the response is complete.

Securing Cargo

Cargo must be properly secured at all times during transport. Proper securement of cargo prevents the load from leaking, spilling, shifting, or falling from the vehicle. A properly secured load must remain secured in all directions to protect against forces reasonably expected to occur during normal driving.

Drivers are responsible for:
+ Inspecting all loads for proper cargo securement prior to initial transport, then re-inspect the cargo within the first 50 miles, again at every duty status change, and every 150 miles or 3 hours of driving (whichever comes first)
+ Securing all cargo not already properly secured

Vehicle and Cargo Security / Key Control

+ All unattended vehicles must be properly parked with the engine shut off, brakes set, and keys removed – this includes customer vehicles, vendor vehicles, and organization-owned and operated vehicles
+ Any vehicle left running while unattended is prohibited
+ Never leave vehicle keys inside parked equipment under any circumstances
+ Ensure all parked equipment is locked when unattended
+ Place only one set of keys on the keyboard or in the lock box
+ Vehicle keys are to remain in the possession of the driver (if remaining on premises), otherwise secured in a designated location inside the facility

+ Ensure that cargo doors are secured (if applicable), seals are in place, and that uncoupled trailers are secured with the kingpin or other suitable locking mechanisms
+ Do not park vehicles at locations that encourage unauthorized entry or damage

Side Guards & Truck Skirts

Larger trucks should be equipped with the appropriate side guards. Side guards are installed to protect other vehicles should they collide with the truck. By installing side guards, when a vehicle that collides with an equipped truck, the side guard should prevent it from going any further rather than shearing off the top of the vehicle.

Truck side guards are vehicle-based safety devices designed to keep pedestrians, bicyclists, and motorcyclists from being run over by a large truck's rear wheels in a side-impact collision.

Drivers shall:
+ Not attempt to modify the side guards or truck skirts – doing so will void the manufacturer's warranty
+ Never use the side guards or truck skirts as a stepladder or use for climbing the truck
+ Not install side guards or truck skirts – only trained maintenance professionals may install for proper modification and to prevent any damage to electrical or other components

Rear Underride Guards

Larger trucks should be equipped with the appropriate rear underride guard. Truck underride crashes could be more survivable to passengers and drivers of smaller vehicles with the effective rear underride guards.

Drivers should:

+ Inspect the rear underride guard certification label, ensure it is clearly able to be seen
+ Look for rust, bending, or loosened fasteners and notify maintenance immediately if any defects or damages are found

Pre-Trip and Post-Trip Responsibility

Pre-Trip CSA Inspection

When conducting a CSA or pre-trip inspection, the driver should:
+ Ensure that their inspection is in compliance with FMCSR Part 396.13 and 392.7(a)
+ Validate that the previous Driver Vehicle Inspection Reports (DVIR) results have all been addressed and remedied to ensure the vehicle is safe to operate (excluding any listed defects on a

towed unit that is no longer part of the vehicle combination)

Drivers must operate in compliance with the following CSA related items:

+ Hold a valid CDL license
+ Valid CDL Endorsements for the vehicle being operated
+ Required PPE
+ Permits are current and present
+ Valid medical card/certification
+ Annual inspection sticker and inspection report is current and legible
+ Vehicle registration plate and matching certificate are present and match the VIN for that vehicle
+ Certificate of Insurance is current and present
+ Certificate of lease or a copy of the lease agreement must be kept in the vehicle
+ Prior logs for the previous seven days and/or OBC instruction card is available
+ All identification items are visibly in place including organization name, address, DOT number on

both sides of the tractor, unit number and fuel decals
+ A signed report for "Driver's Acknowledgement Out" field to certify that defects or deficiencies noted by the driver who prepared the report were repaired and certified by a maintenance technician

Post-Trip Inspection

When conducting a Post-Trip Inspection report, the driver should:
+ Confirm that a DVIR form is being used when defects are found during an inspection (unless the organization only operates one power unit or unless otherwise required)

On the DVIR that lists defects, the driver must:

- + Complete information on vehicle identification such as tractor and trailer(s) numbers
- + Carrier name
- + Driver's name
- + Location number
- + Date and time the workday started
- + Mileage at the conclusion of the workday for that vehicle
- + Ending mileage where the driver is no longer pulling a trailer

On the DVIR, drivers must check the applicable box next to any part or accessory listed that they determine will affect the safety of the motor vehicle or result in its mechanical breakdown.

Additionally, drivers should:
- + Indicate what side of the motor vehicle the defect is on
- + Provide remarks outlining the defects
- + Include specific trailer numbers for all trailers that were used

+ If no defects or deficiencies are known, then this should be indicated in the DVIR
+ Sign the report in the driver signature field (if required to complete a DVIR)

Pre-Documented Post-Trip Inspection

To comply with FMCSR Part 396.11, drivers must complete a post-trip inspection. This regulation requires that drivers document the condition of each motor vehicle they have operated in any given day that contains defects. The report covers the following critical parts and accessories:

+ Broken or missing lighting equipment or reflectors
+ Service brakes, including trailer brake connections
+ Steering mechanisms
+ Tires
+ Horn
+ Rear vision mirrors

- + Windshield wipers
- + Wheels and rims
- + Coupling device
- + Emergency equipment

Other Circumstances

Two-Driver Operations – Only one driver needs to sign the DVIR if it contains defects.

Drivers Operating Multiple Vehicles – A driver who operates multiple vehicles in one day must complete an inspection for each vehicle. If the vehicle contains defects, a post-trip inspection report / DVIR must be completed.

Drivers Operating in Canada – Must document both the pre-trip and post-trip. Separate DVIRs must be completed for the tractor and the trailer. In Canada, drivers must have four DVIRs for each day they operate. Additionally, the time of the inspection must be noted on each DVIR.

Process For Vehicle Repairs

FMCSR and the Ministry of Transportation (MOT) require motor carriers to repair any items listed on the DVIR that could affect the safe operation of that vehicle.

In the event that the DVIR indicates that a repair is necessary, the driver should discuss the repairs with their designated maintenance shop to ensure the shop has a clear understanding of the needed repairs.

Post-Repair Certification

FMCSR and MOT require that when a deficiency or defect is listed on the DVIR. That means that before a vehicle may be dispatched again, the motor carrier must certify the completion of those repairs that were indicated as necessary on the DVIR.

Certification includes:
+ Correction was not needed

- + Deficiency or defect listed on the DVIR has been fixed
- + Vehicle must be placed out-of-service

The maintenance technician makes this certification by signing and dating the DVIR.

Retention

The retention process is required for 90 days for a DVIR that contains defects.

Roadside Inspections

Roadside inspections are required to be kept for 12 months.

Vehicle Safety Procedures

Entering or Exiting Vehicle Cabs And Trailers

When climbing into a vehicle cab, individuals should:

+ Look for water, ice, snow, or oil on the steps, grab bars, and floor – clean or clear off before stepping up
+ Secure two firm handholds on the grab bars on either side of your body – this will assist you with the climb
+ Always maintain at least three solid points of contact while climbing
+ Step up on the first step, placing your foot firmly onto the step. Next, bring your second foot up, placing it firmly next to the other (double foot accommodation step) – if the initial step is a single foot step, then raise the other foot to the next step
+ Before attempting to move to the next handhold position, ensure both feet are planted firmly on an intermediate step
+ Move one hand at a time to maintain a secure handhold while climbing

+ Finally, lift your body one foot at a time onto the cab floor and slide into the vehicle seat
+ Always lean slightly into the vehicle when climbing up or down
+ Never attempt to climb while holding anything in your hands

When climbing out of a vehicle, individuals should:
+ Always face the vehicle
+ Always lean into the vehicle when climbing down or up
+ Always maintain three points of contact
+ Familiarize yourself with the location of all handholds, steps, and any debris that may have accumulated during transport
+ Secure two firm handholds on either side of the body, maintaining at least one firm grip while lowering the other hand
+ Lower down the steps one foot at a time, while maintaining one firmly planted foot until the other foot has been lowered below, then

bringing the upper foot down to meet the other to the same step
+ Ensure both feet are secured on an intermediate step before attempting to move to the next handhold position
+ Finally, lower your body carefully one foot at a time onto the ground, ensuring feet are firmly planted before releasing handhold positions

When entering or exiting a trailer, the following considerations need to be addressed:
+ Inspect the steps and grab bars to ensure they are in good operating condition
+ Do not use inappropriate mechanisms as climbing aids, this includes door closing straps or cargo
+ If physical limitations make climbing too difficult or dangerous then use a platform

ladder or A-frame step ladder for a safe entry and exit
+ Minimize the number of times necessary to climb and exit the trailer by considering the positioning of cargo to make it easier to unload from the ground
+ Avoid walking backwards in the rear of the vehicle
+ Always be aware of your position in relation to the end of the tailgate to avoid accidentally stepping off of the edge
+ Any elevated work on trailers requires the use of an A-frame step ladder or a platform – extension or straight ladders are prohibited
+ Never jump from the vehicle

General Ladder Usage and Vehicular Access

+ Always face the ladder while climbing
+ Familiarize yourself with the operation and location of

available steps that are on your vehicle or trailer

+ Use specialized ladders for the purpose of access or egress from the deck of a flatbed trailers
+ Consult your supervisor for additional information

Lift Gate Safety

+ <u>Never allow children around the truck, lift gate or ramp</u>
+ Always inspect the lift gate for missing or broken pins prior to use
+ During folding and unfolding of the lift gate, stand clear of the gate's path
+ Ensure all other people are clear of the lift gate platform while folding or unfolding
+ Do not ever attempt to catch a lift gate during unfolding or folding
+ Never place any part of your body between the rails and rear of the vehicle

- Never place any part of your body within the equipment's pinch points
- Pinch points occur when a moving part of a machine or other equipment contacts or rubs against another part or surface
- Never place any part of your body between the back of the platform and the rear of the vehicle
- NEVER crawl under the platform of the lift gate when it's raised, whether it is loaded or not
- Inspect the platform for a clean working surface
- DO NOT ATTEMPT REPAIRS ON THE LIFT GATE – only trained technicians are authorized to repair the lift gate
- When in the back of the truck, on the lift gate, or ramp be sure to place close attention so that you do not mistakenly step off and avoid walking backwards
- Have bystanders stay away from the lift gate and ramp to avoid injury from falling loads when in use

- + Never overload the lift gate
- + Never try to catch a falling load –
  attempting to catch a falling load
  could result in an injury
- + Thoroughly read and follow the
  manufacturer's guidelines for safe
  lift gate operations

Starting or Parking the Vehicle

- + Employees, contractors, and
  visitors are not permitted to start
  up or operate a vehicle while not
  properly seated
- + The keys must be removed when
  the vehicle is parked
- + The use of wheel chocks and
  under the steering axle tires are
  required to ensure the safe and
  secured parking position
- + Vehicles with automatic
  transmissions must be in "Neutral"
  or "Park"
- + Vehicles with a manual
  transmission must be in "Neutral"
  with the parking brake engaged

+ Ensure the vehicle's steering wheel is in a position that points the tires straight ahead

Cruise Control

+ Drivers must maintain a safe driving distance at all times (minimum of four to six seconds, depending on the type of vehicle)
+ Add additional seconds and space for adverse weather conditions – for rain add at least one second, for snow add at least two seconds
+ Cruise control should never be engaged in hilly or winding terrain and never in adverse weather conditions
+ Cruise control may only be used on rural interstate / limited access type highways with good, clear visibility and limited traffic
+ The operating speed of vehicles through the highway entrance and exit ramps should always be a minimum of 15mph less than the

posted speed limit and reduced even more as other conditions warrant

+ The operating speed of vehicles through construction zones should also always be a minimum of 15mpg less than the posted speed limit and reduced as other conditions warrant

Seat Belts

Drivers and passengers are required to be seated while riding on the vehicle and must wear proper seat and shoulder belts. The use of bunk restraints are required when in the sleeper. Failure to wear the proper restraints will result in corrective action including up to termination.

Unauthorized Passengers

Unauthorized passengers include pets, relatives, friends, customers, and even other employees that do not have proper authorization for the drive. Any passengers riding in vehicles are required to have written approval on file with the organization prior to the trip.

Cell Phones and Texting

Cell phone use while driving is strictly prohibited. Drivers are expected to abide by all applicable laws regarding cell phone use while driving and all employees are expected to abide by all of the following guidelines while driving a organization vehicle:

+ Drivers may not touch their cell phone while the vehicle is in motion, unless to make an emergency call to report driving hazards or an erratic driver – if possible, pull over prior to making the call
+ All mobile phones used for the purpose of doing business must have voicemail enabled and available for client's to leave a message to be returned when not driving

+ The use of hands-free devices are permitted when the vehicle is moving

Radar Detectors

The use of radar or laser detectors are forbidden in all organization vehicles. Drivers found using radar detectors will have their driving privileges revoked. In many cases, the use of radar detectors in commercial vehicles is illegal.

Headlights

Headlights should remain lit at all times to increase your visibility to other drivers.

Safe Backing

Whenever possible, avoid backing up. In cases where backing is required, then drivers should remember the GOAL (**Get Out And Look)** method. Prior to beginning a backing maneuver, drivers should:

+ Check around the vehicle for tree limbs, awnings, and overhead cables
+ Park in an area that doesn't require backing up out of a parking spot, but instead try to park in areas that allow you to pull out of a spot in a forward direction
+ Engage four way flashers while backing and while stopped for deliveries
+ Physically check all sides of the vehicle for clearance behind, overhead, underneath, both sides, and in the front
+ Use traffic cones/beacons to better facilitate checking of clearances and mark the intended path of travel to serve as markers or to block traffic
+ Turn off the radio and roll down your windows for audible attention
+ Prior to backing up, tap your horn twice to indicate a rear maneuver
+ When using a spotter, keep them in your eyesight at all times – as a

driver you are responsible for
their safety

+ Repeat these steps as many times
that are necessary to safely back
up

U-Turns

A u-turn maneuver exposes commercial
vehicles to greatly increased risks of
collisions with property and other
drivers. U-turn maneuvers are strictly
prohibited.

Security Rules

General

Any employee regarding instances of
workplace harassment, intimidation,

threats, violence, or theft will result in corrective action up to termination.

If you witness any unethical or illegal conduct including dishonesty, you must report this to your supervisor and/or a human resources representative immediately.

Security While Driving

We recommend that drivers abide by the following guidelines to ensure their safety:

+ Communicate with your supervisor daily and report anything out of the ordinary
+ Be conscious of your surroundings and anything that doesn't look right
+ Always remove the keys from the ignition, lock the vehicle, and keep keys in your personal possession for the duration of all stops
+ Avoid unauthorized or unscheduled stops

+ Try to park in well-lit areas designated for commercial vehicles and where other drivers are present
+ Be alert to other drivers that may be following your vehicle, particularly after departing a distribution facility
+ When possible, vary your operating times and route
+ Do not pick up hitchhikers or allow unauthorized passengers into the vehicle at anytime
+ If on a team drive, leave your vehicle one at a time to ensure it is supervised
+ Do not drive the organization's vehicle to your home or any other personal residence
+ Never leave the vehicle unattended in unsecured parking areas
+ Be alert to unknown individuals who appear to be watching or filming vehicles or warehouse operations
+ Keep your cab and access panels locked at all times with the

windows rolled all the way and completely up
+ Unattended vehicles that are not in use must have keys stored in a secured lox box or in the operation's office in a securely locked room or cabinet

Security During Energy Control Procedures

+ Follow the Energy Control (lockout, tag out, blockout) procedures whenever preparing for equipment service or maintenance activities – the unexpected startup or release of stored energy could result in personal injury or property damage
+ Never remove the lock tag, unless you are explicitly authorized to do so

- + Never attempt to startup a vehicle or other piece of equipment that is locked out or tagged out of service
- + Never get underneath or work on a vehicle that does not have they key properly locked and tagged out, parking brake set, wheel chocks placed on a non-drive axle

Security During Vehicle Maintenance

While entering a maintenance facility, drivers should:
- + Use a maximum speed of 5mph
- + Drive cautiously
- + Never enter a restricted work area unless escorted by a maintenance employee
- + Perform a thorough pre-trip inspection to ensure that all safety-related defects are repaired
- + Document all known vehicle defects on the DVIR in a post-trip inspection

+ Never attempt to use a duplicate
  key to start a vehicle that is being
  serviced in a maintenance facility

While fueling, drivers should:
+ Observe and comply with all
  posted regulatory signage
+ Check clearances and know where
  pedestrians are at all times
+ Remain with the vehicle at all
  times during fueling or servicing

How to Influence Sustained Behavioral Change

There are many ways to motivate
people to adjust their behavior, but it is
important to recognize that simply
adopting one of these factors will not

be enough to impact every person on your team.

To appeal to as much of your team as possible, maximize your accountability programs. It is one thing to give your team this handbook and expect them to read through it and abide by it, but to really ensure your team is following through and including these concepts daily, accountability and positive reinforcement are critical.

Here are the most common motivational influencers that change habits:

+ Recognition
+ Competition
+ Savings
+ Fame
+ Giving
+ Passion

Safety Gamification

Driving can often feel like a bit of a game where the rules are centered around being first and getting to your destination faster, but through gamification we can change the rules of the game.

Many fleets are already equipped with technology that compiles information about our commercial drivers including their speed, braking, phone use and other information that can be used more than just for enforcement of driver policies. Instead, we can use positive reinforcement to curb driver behaviors.

In fact, on average when gamification is added to training programs they took 50% less time to complete and organizations are increasing profit margins by about 40% – bottom line, gamifying safe driving tools improves driving conditions and is better for business.

Instead of simply applying a score to a driver's abilities, turn the data into a competitive score where they can track their performance across the fleet and reward drivers both psychologically and organizationally by recognizing their improvements over time and safest drivers. This is an unbiased way of rewarding the organization's safest drivers.

Here is an example of what gamification can look like on a driver's device:

Additionally, there are already apps available for organizations looking to reward their employees for safer driving habits and the best part about it is that it isn't just for commercial drivers. These tools can also help shape your employee's ordinary driving habits, which keeps them healthy and stimulates the local economies.

Pace Car Programs

Another great way to influence both your own fleet's behaviors and the general community is to back a local pace car program.

Community safe-driving pace car programs have been popping up across America. Initially launched in Boise, Idaho by David Engwicht the pace car program was designed to be a "citizen-based initiative" to work in coordination with other initiatives geared towards making roadways safer for everyone. The Federal Highway Administration describes the program in these terms: "Resident pace car drivers agree to drive courteously, at or below the speed limit, and follow other traffic laws. Programs usually require interested residents to register as a pace car driver, sign a pledge to abide by the rules, and display a sticker on their vehicle."

Studies conducted in Columbia, Missouri have determined that Pace Car programs have reduced average speeds from 30 mph to 25 mph. The Transportation Laboratory estimates "that each one mph reduction in average traffic speed provided a reduction of 6% in vehicle accidents for urban main roads and residential roads."

Reported benefits of the pace car programs:
+   Pace Cars generally slow down traffic which is good news! Speeding is the cause of 29% of fatal crashes
+   The Pace Car signs communicate your intentions to other drivers as you model courtesy and safe driving
+   The signage has been shown to reduce road rage towards registered courteous drivers

+ "It puts the responsibility to drive responsibly back on us – the motorists – instead of on our government the police or the traffic engineers. It doesn't require physical traffic calming structures such as speed bumps and chicanes. This not only saves money, but also is easier for emergency vehicles."

Organizations looking to highlight the safety of their fleet can benefit from partnering with local communities in implementing a low-cost pace car program.

Benefits for organizations interested in sponsoring a pace car program:
+ Increased marketing and community awareness of your organization
+ Boosts employee morale
+ Qualify for tax deductions

+   Gives back to the community around you

How are communities launching pace car programs? Fortunately, the Pace Car Programs alleviate the burden for our government, but it will take some collaboration and support to kick off the program.

This relatively low-cost solution will require some basic adjustments to information found on already existing community websites and in local resource centers. The burden on the community is low to zero cost if they are sponsored by private organizations, but low cost should the community choose to launch the program utilizing an existing budget.

How to Reduce Commercial Insurance Premium Hikes & Why You Can't Afford to Wait

Commercial insurance premiums have been on a significant increase as of recently and much of this is being led by employer safety programs that are unable to effectively influence and instruct their employees. As quoted on BusinessInsurance.com, according to New York-based chief broking officer at Aon PLC, Brian S. Wanat, "With each passing month, rates have gone up more. We're looking preliminarily at Q3 being greater than Q2 and we see it gaining momentum at this point," he said. "I think everything outside of workers comp is going up double digits right now, certainly for the larger accounts." Furthermore, David Perez, Liberty Mutual's Chief Underwriting Officer, North America, for Global Risk Solutions, says that "For large risks, some property accounts are seeing 30% or 40% increases."

Every broker has probably been asked for tips and ways that organizations can minimize these inevitable increases and the most common response they give is for organizations to create safety programs that have a trackable impact in reducing incidents. Unfortunately, that is about the extent of the answer and by the time the organizations human resources team puts together an even more robust employee guide equipped with fancy videos and quizzes or badges of achievement, they aren't really impacting the total culture of their workplace. The root of the problem lies within the organization's culture and within each individual's personal motivators, which is why most organizations tend to miss the mark.

What does it take to persuade your commercial insurance provider that your organization is taking serious precautions to limit risk to reduce the increase? First off, the lowest hanging fruit to reduce risk is to address the safety around your employees representing you on the road. Whether they be commercial drivers or your outside sales reps or the managers overseeing them, road safety is the leading and one of the most costly contributing factors to premium increases. In fact, according to an article by CoverHound, Cambridge Mobile Telematics found phone distraction is now the root cause of some 52% of car crashes. Meanwhile, the frequency of collision claims has also skyrocketed in the U.S. over the past several years. This has auto insurance companies experiencing record payouts and according to an article by Forbes, distracted driving could boost your insurance rates by as much as 41%. The concern for your employees driving safely doesn't just stop when they clock out, but their driving habits can impact your bottom line when they are off the clock too. In 2016, nearly 4.6 million drivers and passengers were seriously injured due to distracted driving, the cost of losing a valuable member of your team impacts morale and in many cases requires your organization to fill a role with limited time and resources.

How can your organization take the necessary steps to influence safer driving habits for all employees on the road? It isn't enough to roll out more comprehensive trainings and guidelines, but fortunately employers have numerous technologies that can be easily leveraged to customize your approach for each individual and for less of an investment than the cost of not taking the initiative. A common misconception for some is that these technologies are used to "spy" on employees, but the reality is that when these tools are leveraged properly employers are better equipped to tailor training and motivate each individual rather than applying a one-sized-fits-all approach that has been proven to be less effective.

Here are a few technologies that when applied can help motivate employees to drive safer both on and off the clock:

1. While driving on company time, implement telematics systems for all employees and contractors that drive for in any capacity on behalf of your organization. Look for systems that monitor harsh braking, rapid acceleration, excessive speed, and most importantly handheld and hands-free device use. When implementing this technology be sure to include not only repercussions and actionable steps for repeat offenders, but create an incentive program that truly rewards good behavior.

2. Leverage technologies such as SAFE 2 SAVE that already has incentive programs that can be used both on and off of the clock and on both personal and work phones. Remember, there are six motivational factors to consider

when wanting to change behavior, not everybody is motivated by the same things so it is important that the programs that hit each of these. Ask yourself the following questions: Will this program help my employees financially? Does this program inspire them? Will they feel like they are making a difference? Will they be recognized for their hard work in changing their behavior? Will more competitive employees have opportunity to flex their competitive nature? How will our corporate communications adjust to support the achievements of our employees?

3. Create a safer in-vehicle experience by leveraging tech that can actually block device-use within the vehicle, such as the SafeDrivePod. These pods are great for company phones, but can also be integrated with other technologies and may be good for up to two devices per vehicle. This

can be great for managers (and even loved ones) that find themselves wanting to text or call their employees while they may be out driving during their shift. The employees will receive their messages when their drive has been completed, allowing them to drive distraction-free.

When it comes to reviewing your commercial insurance and your bottom line, consider that the ASSE published a survey of financial decision-makers and the average perceived return on safety investment was $4.41 for every dollar spent on safety, find the full report in the resources segment of this book. Not only do safety programs make smart business sense and benefit the health of your organization, safer practices influence the economy on a grand scale. According to the NHTSA, approximately 7% of all motor vehicle crash costs are paid from public revenues. Federal revenues accounted for 4% and States and localities paid for approximately 3%. An additional 1%

is from programs that are heavily subsidized by public revenues, but for which the exact source could not be determined. Private insurers pay approximately 54% of all costs. Individual crash victims pay approximately 23% while third parties such as uninvolved motorists delayed in traffic, charities, and health care providers pay about 16%. Overall, those not directly involved in crashes pay for over three-quarters of all crash costs, primarily through insurance premiums, taxes and congestion related costs such as travel delay, excess fuel consumption, and increased environmental impacts. In 2010 these costs, borne by society rather than by crash victims, totaled over $187 billion and continues to grow year over year. According to the CDC, for crashes that occurred in 2017, the cost of medical care and productivity losses associated with occupant injuries and deaths from motor vehicle traffic crashes exceeded $75 billion. It is for this reason that hospital systems nationwide too, are anxious to get employers and individuals to address the present dangers on our roadways.

Resources

Vision Zero Network, Retrieved from
https://visionzeronetwork.org/resources
/

Sharpen, A. B. (2017, May 9) *The Need for
(Safe) Speed: 4 Surprising Ways Slower
Driving Creates Better Cities.* Retrieved
from
https://www.wri.org/blog/2017/05/need-s
afe-speed-4-surprising-ways-slower-driv
ing-creates-better-cities

U.S. Department of Transportation
Federal Highway Administration (2010,
May) *Highway Finance Data Collection.*
Retrieved from
https://www.fhwa.dot.gov/policyinformat
ion/pubs/hf/pl11028/chapter4.cfm

Sawicki, D. (2015, November 30) *Braking Factors*. Retrieved from https://copradar.com/redlight/factors/

Jaillet, J. (2013, February 13) *80 percent of car-truck crashes caused by car drivers, ATA report says*. Retrieved from https://www.ccjdigital.com/80-percent-of-car-truck-crashes-caused-by-car-drivers-ata-report-says/

Walker, A. (2017, July 28) *U.S. traffic death increase caused by speeding, says new study*. Retrieved from https://www.curbed.com/2017/7/28/16051780/us-traffic-death-speeding-statistics-speeding

Zetlin, M. (2019, August 21) *5 Ways Even Good Drivers Make Traffic Jams Worse*. Retrieved from https://www.inc.com/minda-zetlin/holiday-traffic-jams-better-flowing-traffic-driving-techniques-tailgating-left-lane-driving.html

Simmons, S. (2019, August 26) *Pay attention: Want to see what it looks like to speed in a school zone?* Retrieved from https://www.khou.com/video/news/local/htownrush/pay-attention-want-to-see-what-it-looks-like-to-speed-in-a-school-zone/285-8db25b85-b082-44b2-b74a-6ca5995e2813

Kamal, T. (2017, June 1) *Fleets Make Streets Safer with Vision Zero Initiative.* Retrieved from https://www.government-fleet.com/157450/fleets-make-streets-safer-with-vision-zero-initiative

U.S. Department of Transportation Volpe Center (2019, June 6) *Truck Side Guards Resource Page.* Retrieved from https://www.volpe.dot.gov/our-work/truck-side-guards-resource-page

Bradt, G (2013, July 10) *How Salesforce And Deloitte Tackle Employee Engagement With Gamification.* Retrieved from https://www.huffpost.com/entry/how-salesforce-and-deloit_b_3539563

DeMarco, G. (2011, July 25) *Minority Rules: Scientists Discover Tipping Point for the Spread of Ideas.* Retrieved from https://news.rpi.edu/luwakkey/2902

Rossy, G.M., Sun, C.C., Jessen, D., Newman, E. (2008) *Residential Speed Limit Reduction Case Studies.* Retrieved from http://engineers.missouri.edu/csun/files/2016/08/Residential_Speed_Limit_MU_Springfield.pdf

U.S. Department of Transportation Federal Highway Administration (2019, April 1) *A Resident's Guide for Creating Safer Communities for Walking and Biking.* Retrieved from https://safety.fhwa.dot.gov/ped_bike/ped_cmnity/ped_walkguide/

The Salt Lake City Neighborhood Pace
Car Program (2000, September)
Retrieved from
http://www.slcdocs.com/transportation/
TrafficManagement/PDF/pace2000.pdf

The City of Columbus (2019) *Pace Car
F.A.Q.* Retrieved from
https://www.columbus.gov/Templates/D
etail.aspx?id=2147488124

Township of Nutley (2019) *Pace Car
Challenge.* Retrieved from
https://www.columbus.gov/Templates/D
etail.aspx?id=2147488124

St. Louis, M. (2016, September 13) *4 Ways
That Supporting Charity Is Good for
Business.* Retrieved from
https://www.inc.com/molly-reynolds/4-w
ays-that-supporting-charity-is-good-for
-business.html

Karth, M. (2019, February 19) *CVSA Responds to Senators' Request to Add Rear Underride Guards to Vehicle Inspection Checklist.* Retrieved from https://annaleahmary.com/2019/02/cvsa -responds-to-senators-request-to-add-r ear-underride-guards-to-vehicle-inspec tion-checklist/

Road to Zero (2018, July 26) *Safety Priority Statement Comprehensive Underride Protection.* Retrieved from https://www.nsc.org/Portals/0/Documen ts/DistractedDrivingDocuments/Driver- Tech/Road%20to%20Zero/Truck-Underr ide-Priority-Statement.pdf?ver=2018-06-2 6-110039-407

Truck Safety Coalition (2017, August 10) *Tag: Rear Underride Guards.* Retrieved from http://trucksafety.org/tag/rear-underri de-guards/

Gavin Souter (2019, October 15), *Commercial insurance prices set to keep rising into 2020*. Retrieved from https://www.businessinsurance.com/article/20191015/NEWS06/912331151/Commercial-insurance-prices-set-to-keep-rising-into-2020

CoverHound (2017, December 11), *Is Distracted Driving Affecting Commercial Auto Insurance Premiums*. Retrieved from https://coverhound.com/insurance-learning-center/is-distracted-driving-affecting-commercial-auto-insurance-premiums

Jim Gorzelany (2018, April 10), *Pay Attention: Distracted Driving Could Boost Your Insurance Rates By As Much As 41%*. Retrieved from https://www.forbes.com/sites/jimgorzelany/2018/04/10/pay-attention-distracted-driving-could-boost-your-insurance-rates-by-as-much-as-41/#277857bd3c86

Haley Bass (2018, March 26), *The Workplace Cost of Distracted Driving.* Retrieved from https://www.concentra.com/resource-center/articles/the-workplace-cost-of-distracted-driving/

ASSE: Huang, Y.-H., Leamon, T.B., Courtney, T.K., DeArmond, S., Chen, P.Y., Blair, M.F (Published 2009), *Financial Decision Makers' Views on Safety: What SH&E Professionals Should Know.* Retrieved from https://www.tib.eu/en/search/id/BLSE%3ARN248501606/Financial-Decision-Makers-Views-on-Safety-What/

NHTSA (2015, May), *The Economic and Societal Impact Of Motor Vehicle Crashes, 2010 (Revised).* Retrieved from https://crashstats.nhtsa.dot.gov/Api/Public/ViewPublication/812013

CDC (2019, August 14), *Cost Data and Prevention Policies*. Retrieved from https://www.cdc.gov/motorvehiclesafety /costs/index.html

Author – AJ T. Cole

AJ T. Cole is an author, speaker, and road safety advocate that has worked on Vision Zero and road safety initiatives across the United States. AJ has been touched by the big truck industry since youth and comes from a family that both owned and operated big trucks. Safety always being a centerpoint of focus. Commercial driving and managing employees on the roads sets the pace for communities everywhere and impacts the economy on a grand scale.

AJ T. Cole works with organizations and communities to address transportation safety issues and influence the change in behavior behind the wheel.

Interested in seeking AJ's help making your organization safer? AJ can help.

@AJTCole
ajtcole@gmail.com

www.ingramcontent.com/pod-product-compliance
Lightning Source LLC
Chambersburg PA
CBHW030648220526
45463CB00005B/1691